1 MONTH OF
FREE
READING

at

www.ForgottenBooks.com

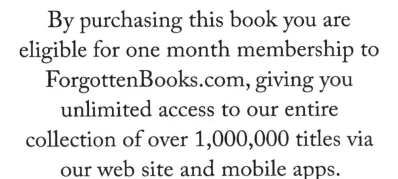

By purchasing this book you are eligible for one month membership to ForgottenBooks.com, giving you unlimited access to our entire collection of over 1,000,000 titles via our web site and mobile apps.

To claim your free month visit:

www.forgottenbooks.com/free781870

ISBN 978-0-484-40150-0
PIBN 10781870

THE
GLEANER

HARVEST·ISSUE

The Gleaner

Official Organ of the Student Body
Entered at The Farm School Post Office as second class matter.
Subscription, $2.00 per year.

VOL. XXXIIII   OCTOBER ISSUE, 1929   No. 8

THE STAFF

Editor-in-Chief
MILTON WERRIN

Business Manager   *Secretary*
KENNETH COLEMAN, '30   SIDNEY GOLDBERG, '30

DEPARTMENTS

Literary   *Campus News*   *Agriculture*
JOSEPH E. BERMAN, '30   CARL COHEN, '31   BERNARD GAYMAN, '31
                                      E. PETKOV, '30

Alumni   *Athletics*   *Exchange*
ABRAHAM RELLIS, '30   THEODORE KRAUSE, '30   SAMUEL MARCUS, '30

Art
WILLIAM FISHER, '30   ALEX. KRICHEF, '32 *Ass't.*

FACULTY ADVISERS
MR. PAUL McKOWN, *Literary Adviser*   MR. SAMUEL B. SAMUELS, *Business Adviser*

CONTENTS

ABRAHAM ERLANGER

*A*BRAHAM ERLANGER, well-known philanthropist and patron of the National Farm School and many other educational and public welfare institutions, died suddenly, October 1st, in his apartments at the Warwick Hotel, New York. He was 74 years of age and unmarried. A brother, Charles Erlanger, survives him.

Deceased was born December 4, 1855, in Lancaster, Pa., the son of Simon and Yetta (Gump) Erlanger. He was graduated from the Lancaster High School and began his business career in Iowa, later removing to Baltimore, where he engaged in the clothing manufacturing business. He had been a resident of New York since 1893.

Since his retirement from active business, Mr. Erlanger had devoted his time to philanthropic activities. He had been chairman of the National Farm School expansion project since 1925, president of the Society for the Welfare of the Jewish Deaf in New York, director of the Institution for Improved Instruction of Deaf Mutes, and had, as executor of the estate of Rosetta Ulman, of Wilkes-Barre, made donations to various Jewish institutions and aided in the publication of the Margolis-Marx History of the Jews, issued by the Jewish Publication of America.

Funeral services were held yesterday morning at the Free Synagogue House in New York. Among Philadelphians present were Mr. Herbert D. Allman, president, and Mr. Joseph H. Hagedorn, vice-president of the National Farm School.

A Tribute to

ABRAHAM ERLANGER

By PRESIDENT ALLMAN

*A*BRAHAM ERLANGER needs no eulogy from me. His many deeds of human kindness; his benevolent impulse to aid all endeavors, charitable, educational and philanthropic; his loving personality and countless friends who endearingly called him "Uncle Abe", speak more eloquently than words of tongue or pen.

It was a privilege to know this good man of so many virtues, whose friendship, advice and counsel were most uplifting and beneficial. His was a noble character, modest, unselfish and generous. He had unbounded faith in his fellowman, never speaking nor harboring ill-will toward anyone. All these qualities, in addition to his sweet guilelessness, endeared him to those who knew, loved and worked with him. They appreciated his loyalty, knew that his spirit rang true, that his motives were altruistic, that his heart, as well as his hand governed his desire to help humanity. He disliked prominence or publicity, quietly giving away fortunes with the understanding his name should be withheld. It was with much difficulty we finally persuaded him to allow the use of his name on the model Dairy Barns and valuable 350-acre tracts of land he donated, now known as the "Erlanger Farms".

The future will continue to show the beneficial results and influence that through his means and labor will come to the School he loved. We deeply mourn the loss of our dearly beloved friend and Trustee, Uncle Abe. The School will always remember its generous benefactor—Abraham Erlanger. May God rest his soul in peace—Amen.

MILTON WERRIN, '30   *Editor-in-Chief*

Farm School
An Investment In Manhood

*F*ARM SCHOOL *is admittedly working to train young men to practice the most efficient methods of producing articles of food and clothing necessary to everyone.*

Besides doing this, Farm School does more. In pitching the wheat, cultivating and harvesting the crops, sweating and straining in the sun, we rebuild ourselves in body and mind. New friendships and new facts of life gained in study make a lasting impression upon us. Nature herself, as we observe her works, shows us the ways of life. We would indeed be blind if we could not see them.

As we look back over the past season and as we near the finish of our school career, we are aware of a new strength, a confidence in ourselves and in our ability to face the world. Such is Farm School's Investment in Manhood.

Inchcape

THE world was a panorama to Inchcape, a background of shifting scenes before which action after action in which he had a violent part took place. Had he confined his exploits to one country merely, he would have been a hobo, but he was an adventurer. An adventurer is a cosmopolitan hobo.

Not a strange city in the world but he knew its blind alleys, dark corners, retreats, dens, with the strange creatures who frequented them. Liverpool, Marseilles, London, Frankfort, Oslo, Calcutta, Melbourne, Bangkok, he knew them all, and a thousand others less well known about which he could tell fantastic things, and find his way about on the most rainy, starless night. The lore of wandering he knew, and devious strange ways to get along; had he been less honest he could have been a prince among racketeers, but a perverse rectitude saved him from that. When we add that he was something of a poet, something of a wit, a not indifferent architect, and a confirmed seeker of the new and strange, you know him better than we do, reader, having, we have no doubt, read more romantic stories than we; nevertheless, we knew him in the flesh, and have heard stories bearing the stamp of truth from his own lips.

No less indomitable when I saw him last than in his earlier years Inchcape yet impressed me as less feverish and cynical. Then the world was his oyster, which he would perforce have opened, "had he but a lever long enough". Many times he thought he had this lever, but he always lacked the fulcrum without which no lever is usable. He called these levers philosophies, and the fulcrum, which never seemed to be at his disposal, he had some hazy notion of as Faith.

At one time in his life the panorama was all sea, hardly varied enough from one day to the next to be called a panorama, yet the chronometer proved a constant motion, in which his ship floated. Six years alone on a schooner around the world, a month in the company of every kind of congenial man and woman.

A war next engaged this Inchcape. Savage war. Not a contest between general and general in steel huts miles apart with men for pawns, but a pitting of muscle against muscle, guile against guile, amid weird manifestations of nature in a land torn into peaks and gorges. Here, a life force amid the wreckage of dead forces, he led a little band in the name of liberty against the lords of the country, and was overwhelmed. After privations unendurable, he was back again in his

London, a shadow seeking a body to inhabit.

He preferred London to New York. London had the accumulations of ten hundred years in its favor, an accumulation of dust, holes, and antiquity not to be despised by a lover of spectres. Even London, however, for this first time in his life lacked a vital element. He had never before experienced such an inanity and emptiness. The endless surge of people, their joys and sorrows, the dense fog drifting into alleys and stairways, clinging in droplets to his coat, all sent a shiver as much mental as physical through him. Used to uttering his thoughts aloud in solitude, Inchcape here in the midst of busy London muttered to himself. If the human tide about him had ceased that moment its movements they would have heard one word repeated many times by this outlandish figure. "Cold", was the word he many times repeated in a melancholy voice. For perhaps the first time in his life Inchcape felt a pang of homesickness.

Now every other person in the world who had ever been homesick before, knew what he was sick to see again. There was a man named Payne once who had been sick for home and wrote a song about it which everybody knows how to sing. Other people longed for other things, mostly dim remembrances highly idealized: a child, a brother, a sweetmeat they once had eaten procurable in only one spot on earth, a sweetheart they had left, a house, friends,—even paradises of combinations of these. All these dreams as Inchcape thought of them, only bewildered him the more. Family he had none, the circumstances and place of his birth were mysteries, he called no house home, no land country; and now London couldn't hold him.

A lamp shining through a fog looks very like the sun seen through mist.

Inchcape remembered the sun. He remembered it burning overhead in a copper sky on the Indian Ocean, dimly on the horizon six slow months at Hudson's Bay, and fierce as the open mouth of a furnace at Yucatan. The mist suddenly lifted, and from then on he knew what he wanted.

Striding briskly onward, animated by a sudden decision, he passed the stairs of the building on Newcastle Street which houses the offices of the Canadian Land Grant Commission. Napoleon in a blue coat and white waistcoat and breeches dominated the office. A man not unlike the Corsican in avoirdupois and demeanor here directed destinies behind a walnut desk on which a card designated him as MR. PETER ABERAY. Napoleonic was the interview which followed Inchcape's entrance.

"Mr. Aberay," he said, "I should like to take over a few acres of Canadian homestead to settle."

Mr. Aberay evidently purveyed square miles as unconcernedly as postage stamps, for he took a printed form in one hand and a pen in the other and by deftly interrogating Inchcape while he wrote soon drew up the deed.

"There you are," he said. "Staked. You're welcome, I'm sure. Now when you're in Montreal just show these papers at our office there and they'll fix you up."

What devil possessed Inchcape to secure a God-forsaken waste in Canada to parade his world-weary bones upon he never knew, except that it was one of those divinities the ancients used to worship as the sun. Certain it was that this imp of fate must have loved him very dearly, whatever his name or ultimate form was. The element of luck had been a feature of Inchcape's life in all his wanderings. He had thanked his lucky stars for this and that, but now he knew that these were always stars of the lesser magnitudes. This sun was an Alpha Major, dominating not one constellation only but the whole heavens.

He had never battled adverse winds alone in a battered sloop more intensely, or with a clearer mind than he fought for his grains and his stock. He had never felt attached to earth before at all; here he was patriot of some hundreds of acres. He had never felt so akin to the rest of the world as when he girdled it as he was isolated here on his Canadian ranch. Nature had never appealed to him so or solitude charmed him, as the Nature his possessions bounded, and the winds that swept them, and the solitude these implied. He loved them all. Even humanity, which before he had barely reckoned on as contributary to his existence, now became a reality to him, personified by his distant neighbors and more nearly by his hired men. Daily contact with these, rough as they were, humanized him. He became conscious of something more in the world than mere conflicts. Poetry which before he had enjoyed for the sheer sensual exaltation of it revealed a wealth of life and emotion which he daily grew more capable of absorbing, and books captivated him with strange new elements of beauty. He saw that this new adventure he had espoused as a whim, was the true reaiity, and his wayward former life the whim.

There he lives today in a remote Canadian province, at peace with himself and the world. He has grown a beard, married, increased his lands, and exhibited other stalwart properties. Those who know him like him, including his cows. His men hope he will live long, and so do we; a living example to all vapid romancers and false economists whom farm life surfeits.

"Take my word for it," he says, as though to say, "don't learn as I learned; if you want romance, seek it on a farm. There's more in that than in the compass of the moving pictures, more excitement, vastly more interest. At least, that's my experience. William Blake, the poet, put very nicely into verse what I mean:

'To see a World in a Grain of Sand,
    And a Heaven in a Wild Flower,
Hold Infinity in the palm of your hand,
    And Eternity in an hour.' "

T. S. S.

The changeful autumn will soon be here,
The most beautiful time of all the year,
When field and woods and vale and hill
Are arrayed and painted past man's best skill.

The countryside never looks so fair,
As in the autumn's clean, clear air,
With lazy clouds afloat on high
And air alive with butterflies.

The birds again are southward bound,
Except the crow, whose mournful sound
Through wintry days, a dreary call
Will come from treetops bare and tall.

The harvest time is here again
When nature yields her wealth to men.
The frost is on the pumpkin, gold,
The corn is shocked, and nights grow cold.

What was sown has now been reaped;
On him that sowed, nature has heaped,
From her horn of plenty, a wealth untold,
Worth more than silver, the harvest gold.

KEISER, '31.

As Ye Sow—So Shall Ye Reap

*H*ARVEST*—International in scope, this yearly festival of mankind has, from days immemorial, occupied an important place in the life of the farmer.*

Harvest and the tiller of the soil, having paid his tribute of toil and care to mother earth, was once more ready to reap the product of his labor with a feeling of satisfaction and thanksgiving.

Even as in the days when Israel clung to the labors of the soil, the festival of harvest time emerged into a grand and picturesque affair. Those who had lived by the generosity of the soil assembled within the walls of the Holy City, to bow their heads in gratitude to the Almighty. Also among the Greeks and Romans, and later nations, did the traditional celebration of Harvest become firmly established. It was a necessary and noble outlet for an emotional urge.

Today, and particularly in the United States, the farmer ascribes real significance to harvest only insomuch as this process is connected with material gains. The farmer fails to attach to it the issues of moral importance.

In the days of combines and gas engines, the harvest festival has passed into oblivion. The fact is that mass production and constant competition have merely mechanized the mind of the farmer and fairly well enslaved him. The farmer, it seems, becomes the victim of the cold, heartless iron and steel—the machines without souls. And for this, he has sacrificed something finer, something purer, something nobler. Was it worth while?

Our 32nd Harvest

*L*ONG ago, when the earth had become somewhat solidified, the very first signs of life after the steaming vastness were the plants that sprang from the soil. Since then the soil has continued regularly to send forth its abundance, and is still the source of life, while man, like all other animals, depends upon it for his existence.

When man first came upon the earth, he took of the fruits of the field, but gave nothing in return. Mother Nature knowing man much better than he himself, and being a wise old mother, fortunately decided that no longer would she release the treasure of her soil, unless man made some effort to obtain it. And so we scratch the surface of the earth to a depth of six or seven inches while Mother Nature looks on approvingly, and to him who scratches well and deeply she fills to the brim his cornucopia.

Here at National Farm School, the laws of nature also prevail and having tilled the soil in earnest endeavor, we share the treasures we have unlocked. Our bins have been filled to capacity; 2,000 bushels of wheat in all have been stored away. The yield per acre wasn't so bad at that, averaging twenty bushels. Oats come second with 1200 bushels, averaging twenty-five bushels to the acre. We have harvested three hundred tons of good grade hay, which will possibly carry us through the winter. Our early potato crop has not yielded what we thought it might, but there are good reasons for such results. The early spring rains and continuous dry weather thereafter are partly responsible for the unsuccessful attempt. We picked 150 bushels at that, but the experiment was worth while. Therefore we lay great hopes on our late potato crops. Every-thing is coming along as it should; considering the dry spell, they look fairly good. They have been sprayed a dozen times, and this year we might enter the 600 club, but let's have patience. The silage corn looks good this year; eight to ten tons per acre is something to boast of. As to the field corn which will remain in the field until matured, no estimate can be given yet. We might say that the Home Barn this year succeeded in getting through with its work earlier than in previous years; this is partly due to the new system of early industrials and the co-operation of the Student Body and department heads. All our threshing has practically been finished, due to the efforts of Mr. Groman. The silo is almost filled, and plowing has started. Winter wheat is being seeded at the time these lines are written, and, by the way, you are to know that about 150–180 acres of wheat are going in this year. It wont be long now before we will have to employ combines, as they do out West.

At the Dairy things look fairly bright. The milk flow is steady. Their pasture is running out and is supplemented with extra grain, sweet corn stover and soy bean hay. Fresh silage is also fed.

The pasture land will be reseeded for next year and might be extended over to No. 6 land to give the herd more room. Much progress is achieved in the building up of the herd. Old stock will be sold to accommodate young stock. This year the department has sent down 30 head of cattle to the Doylestown Fair. It is predicted that competition will be much keener this year. Last year we won most of the prizes. Our imported Jerseys, as Whitey Gysling tells me, have completed the test and made good records.

The Ayrshire Heifers are looking good and are now mature for breeding. They expect to purchase a bull soon for this purpose. The Abortion Test is still carried out every three months, but the T.B. test has been deferred until Christmas. The new maternity barn is filled to capacity. The Department had more luck in obtaining heifers than bulls. Just imagine three in one week. And now we will go over to the poultry dep't while we are on the subject of livestock. At the present time they have about 850 laying hens, and about 500 pullets will come in December. The laying percentage is about 50 per cent and the flock is being held back from heavy laying. The birds which have been out on range for the summer, have been taken in. The fact remains that they are far superior to those confined. No trouble from cannibalism or disease has been experienced so far with these birds. For next year seven more range houses will be built, since they proved a success, making a total of ten. The pullets are now being fed a 50 per cent corn meal mash to fatten them up for the laying season. The annual cleaning program is over and completed.

At the Horticulture department it seems they can't get enough help to do the picking. For the last two weeks, peaches were in the spotlight with 1116 baskets and brought in $1045 in cash. Practically all Smokehouse apples have been picked and have sold well. For the remainder of the apple crop they expect to get very good prices this year on account of the cold spell that killed the blossoms in several of the surrounding sections. Several tons of grapes have been harvested from our vineyard. Most of the vegetables are off now, and late crops are making great headway, for example, late cabbage and lettuce are 100 per cent crops. Of our vegetables,

sweet corn, tomatoes, lima beans, and string beans rank first in profit on investment. The pumpkins are coming along fine and some of these also went down to the Doylestown Fair. As soon as the grapes are off, fall plowing will begin. Our asparagus patch of $3\frac{1}{4}$ acres will be also mulched for the winter. The attempted Roadside Market has proven to be a success, considering the short time it has been in operation, for which credit is due to Mr. Purnell and the Horticulture Seniors. According to M. Oros, this year has been more prosperous than the three or four previous years.

The Greenhouses have been painted and given a thorough repairing. This is a treat after such an interval of so many years. They, too, are doing quite a bit of planting and harvesting; 700,000 ivy cuttings are expected to be put in. The beds have been filled with early sweet peas, snap dragons and chrysanthemums. The entire lower house is also occupied with 'mums. Crops coming in, are early 'mums, asters, calla lilies, which come in a month earlier this year, and gladiolas. A new flower, the cyclamen, will be tried this year for the first time. Other new crops grown at our greenhouses this year will be lupines, friesias, colendulas. But above all they will give another crop a chance. Not flowers, this time, but mushrooms. Mr. Mayer will start off on a small scale, but intends to go in bigger if the crop proves worthy. Snap dragons will be put on sale in pots, and the Delphinium will be forced. I'm asked to report that Coleman's mignonettes are still coming up. Give them a chance!! The first thing Russell Broadbent began with was something like this: "Lawn Mowing is a thing of the past. All mowers have been greased up and put away in the shed, until next year. These boys must have developed their

(Continued on page 30)

Extracted Honey

UP TO the year of 1865, extracted honey was practically unknown on the market. Liquid honey offered for sale was obtained from the comb by the process of pressing and straining. This type of honey contained foreign substances such as pollen, wax particles, propolis, bee glue, and some dirt. On the contrary, the liquid honey of today, known as extracted honey, is obtained from the comb by centrifugal force. The honeycombs are placed in a machine with pockets varying in size which revolve around a central rod, thus throwing the honey out. This process keeps the combs in good form and they may be given to bees for continuous use. The honey is free from any foreign matter or dirt, which impairs the flavor.

There are almost as many kinds of honey, varying in flavor, color and body, as there are flowering plants. The light honeys as clover, alfalfa, sage, basswood, orange and many others, are most important for table use. The dark honeys as buckwheat, golden rod, aster and heather (from Scotland) are not so popular, due to the strong flavor; they are used by bakers and confectioners. Products which contain honey, as a rule, keep fresh and wholesome for a longer period of time because of the power honey has in absorbing moisture.

The flavor of extracted honey is often partly or wholly lost by overheating. A natural condition of honey is granulation which is brought about by change of temperatures and also by the large quantity of dextrose present. Honey consists of three sugars, dextrose, levulose and sucrose. The composition of honey is as following; dextrose and levulose of equal amounts, sucrose in a smaller quantity, and water about 16–20 per cent. Honey with a smaller quantity of dextrose will

(Continued on page 23)

STUDENTS WORKING WITH MODERN TRACTION MACHINERY

Do Not Put Off For Tomorrow What You Can Do Today

*T*HE above, I believe, is the key-note of Farm School's success in all sports, being especially true of football. Last year, 11 letter men out of 17 graduated. Such a loss would be sufficient to daunt most men, but not Coach Samuels. With the energy that characterizes everything he does, he immediately set to work reorganizing the squad. All winter fellows could be seen in the gym practicing, and as soon as the weather permitted, they were out on the field.

The first official practice was called for August 3rd, and 43 candidates responded. They have been hard at it for six weeks now, and as a result are in the acme of condition. So confident is Coach Samuels of their ability that he has taken on a game with McKenzie Prep, a school of no mean reputation, for the 29th of September; a week earlier than was previously planned for the first game.

Al Gysling, our captain and foremost guard, rated one of the best who has ever donned a Green and Gold uniform, is looking better than ever. With Al as an incentive, there should be some fine work on the line this year.

Nate Werrin is playing at his old position on end, and is working hard to sustain his reputation as the best tackler and clipper on the team. When Werrin tackles a man, he stays tackled.

Ed Seipp, Al's running mate of last year, has been shifted to center to fill the vacancy left by Rand and Silver of last year. Ed has been practicing diligently since last fall and his excellent passing is showing it.

Jerry Hartenbaum, our versatile and hard playing fullback, is back again kicking better than ever. We almost lost Jerry due to several operations; but he has fully recovered now, and is looking like a million dollars.

Grizzly Grisdale, who made the varsity end in his freshman year through sheer grit and hard playing, is looking better than ever. With last year's experience behind him, Gris should go big this year.

Ken Campbell, who has been plugging hard for two years, has been rewarded by making the guard position. Ken doesn't say much, but he uses his hands a-plenty and is always giving us plenty of action.

Phil Kleinman, a regular of last year until a broken wrist put him out, is back at his old position. Phil has developed into a triple threat man and is circling ends, passing and kicking with a celerity that is a surprise to all.

Fred Rohrbaugh, our 200-pound tackle, and the biggest man on the team, is playing a great game. Fred is mopping up the opposition like nobody's business, and the backs should have no trouble gaining through him.

"Si" Padolin, our lean quarterback, is barking out those signals like a veteran. With "Si" as field general, the team should work together as one, and we're looking forward to a season without any hitches.

Sam Goldfarb, tackle and chief punishment dealer, is covering his territory in fine style. Sam has adopted the slogan, "They Shall Not Pass", and is living up to it to the letter.

Jesse Elson, the big boy of the backfield, and the only freshman to have landed a regular's berth, is showing up as one of the best defensive men on the team. Elson came to school with a rep as a ball player, and is certainly living up to it.

Coach Samuels also has great confidence in his second team. As he once said on the field, "This is the first year in several that I'm able to go to bed without worrying about a first stringer getting hurt, for I know I can replace them with men equally as good," which, I believe, is a real compliment, and the scrubs certainly should feel proud of it.

JUNIORS GAIN THE UPPER HAND IN ANNUAL FRESHMAN-JUNIOR BASEBALL TILT

Lack of space did not permit our publishing this important interclass game in the Alumni Issue.

After giving the Freshies a five-run lead in the first inning the Juniors came back with a crash to win the game, 9–5.

The upper classmen were evidently a bit rattled which, no doubt, accounted for the five runs. In the second inning, however, they settled down and held their opponents scoreless the rest of the game.

The freshmen lacked the necessary batting punch to come through, and thus lost several opportunities to score.

FOOTBALL SCHEDULE—1929

Sept. 28—McKenzie Prep., at Farm School.

Oct. 5—Gettysburg Academy, at Farm School.

Oct. 12—Stevens Trade School, at Farm School.

Oct. 19—Haverford College, Jr. Varsity, at Farm School.

Oct. 26—Temple University High School, at Farm School.

Nov. 2—Susquehanna Univ., Jr. Varsity, at Farm School.

Nov. 9—Drexel Freshmen, at Farm School.

Nov. 16—Central Evening High School, at Farm School.

Nov. 23—Brown Prep., at Farm School.

Nov. 28—(Thanksgiving Day)—Williamson Trade School, at Farm School.

C. COHEN '31   E. PETKOV '30

President's Address to Student Body
Friday, June 28, 1929

ALTHOUGH always busy in the Philadelphia Office, I come to the School today solely for the purpose of addressing you upon the subject of hazing and raiding, certainly a puerile and unmanly practice, which the Trustees and Faculty will insist upon stamping out, for the good of the Institution.

The Board of Trustees endeavor to encourage a proper school spirit, and have no objection to occasional innocent or harmless stunts, when under the supervision of those in charge of the student morale. When, however, unfair and brutal advantage is taken—when an indecent raid is made upon the Freshmen by upper classmen, as was the case a few days ago, it becomes our imperative duty to see that this regrettable procedure never occurs again.

You do not see me very often at the School, nevertheless, I am in daily touch with everything that goes on, and learned of this raid one hour after it happened. Do you think this news was pleasant, or helped to lessen my many responsibilities? There is hardly a lad in this hall whom I have not personally interviewed in a fatherly way when applying for admittance. Therefore, you must be aware from these talks, during which your parents or guardians were present, that the Trustees and the Jewish people who make this great institution possible, have but one thought in mind. We are doing everything in our power to make you comfortable and happy while receiving your training here. We endeavor to give you the best education possible in agriculture—training you morally, mentally and physically, so that you may be a credit to yourselves and your Alma Mater. Take for instance the physical improvements, always going on around you—the contemplated erection of the new Farm Mechanics Building, the first of its kind in the East—the new Administration Offices—the building of new macadam roads—the purchase of imported pure-bred stock—first class dormitories and laboratories and other betterments in view, for which the money is not yet in sight. Don't you think we should have your co-operation and pride in the upbuilding of this Institution, not the tearing down process your late actions may cause? In addition, you are privileged to benefit from the training and instruction given you by an experienced staff of teachers.

I often wonder whether students realize the noble calling in which these men of the Faculty are engaged. Did you ever stop to think of the patience, energy and judgment they must possess and impart—of the long hours and limited pay—of the year in and year out sameness of service rendered? Every Spring, they start all over again with a new Freshman class, whilst you go forth into the world at the end of your three-year term, properly equipped for the vocation you have chosen. Given the opportunity, the members of the Faculty will gladly be your friends and advisers. If you take your problems to them, you will become better and wiser young men. These men and women divide the big responsibility of running this Institution of some 235 souls with the Dean and Trustees of the School. When you enter here, you are no longer under the supervision of your parents or guardians, you become our boys, therefore we become responsible and are as much interested in your moral and ethical training, as in your agricultural education. The only return we ask, is that you succeed in life and become a credit to the School.

Do not accuse me of lecturing, I am trying to help by giving you sound advice, based on many years' experience with boys and educational endeavors. Question the men of the Alumni who will be your guests next week; most of them will tell you of the wonderful progress and improvements made here since they were students, no doubt, including their regret for not having fully appreciated its many benefits, until after years, when actually engaged in the battle of life.

Hazing and raiding will not be tolerated at this Institution. Therefore, those students desiring to take advantage of our free scholarships, will please take notice and govern themselves accordingly. Any and all students found guilty of brutal and unmanly participation in hazing, will be immediately expelled. You know what happened to former student Corr, who failed to heed the several warnings given him. He was finally expelled. The expulsion of another

lad is still being carefully considered before a final decision is made. Notwithstanding great pressure and pleading were brought to bear in Corr's behalf by his parents and friends, he will not be allowed to return to the School. We are sorry for this lad, who otherwise was a good scholar. He seems earnest in his desire to make some branch of agriculture his vocation, and we hope, it will be possible for him to receive his training elsewhere.

We do not claim that ours is the only available agricultural school, but we know of its uniqueness. It is the only Institution of its kind in America where a city-bred lad is given the opportunity to major in both the theory and practice of agriculture; possible here, because of his part time in laboratory, school room and actual practice in field and dairy. The National Farm School is now favorably known throughout these United States among Jews and non-Jews, and I am confident you lads would much rather boost your school than knock it. Applications by the score are daily coming to our office from all over the country, and only the highest type lads can receive our limited free scholarships.

Hazing in schools and colleges has been obsolete for many years, and was never based on logical foundation or reason. School spirit is commendable, but brutality cannot and will not be tolerated. Disciplinary training to lads in their formative years is a most important adjunct to their education—of great service when on their own.

Let me read you a letter received last week from an intelligent mother. Boys need not necessarily air their troubles when home, yet a mother's heart subconsciously senses her boy's unhappiness, even though he be silent:

(*Continued on page 29*)

School Notes

With instructors refreshed by a well-needed vacation and students ready for a change, the classrooms have become the usual scenes of questions, answers, note taking and discussion.

One new course has been added to the curriculum: a senior elective course in Present-Day Government Problems. The Soils and Soil Fertility course has been changed to be given in the Junior year. A new textbook, "Farm Soils"—Worthen —has been obtained for this course. The grind is on.

Jack was going to Atlantic City. Joe was going to New York. Jim was going to New Hampshire. Others went to Ohio. Others nearer, to Philadelphia. Before going there was the usual talk of the good times and how, to come; eats, etc.

Some wanted to make use of the information and practice gained so far and went to work for near-by farmers. Not knowing what conditions they would meet, there was no talk beforehand. On their return, however, talk was plentiful and more interesting than the previous kind, for it was of new and real experiences. There were good bosses and skinflints. There were fine meals and meager ones. Everyone had to "Ring the bell" when on the job. There were record loads made and record unloadings accomplished. Not the least of all the news was that of the gain beside the wages: Seeing how other men farmed to make a living.

The Class of Thirty-One's Junior Prom was held at the spot euphemistically known as Sylvan Dell on Saturday evening, Sept. 7. Of course it rained.

Nevertheless, not a spirit was dampened, except next morning when a hay ride was rashly attempted between showers and the intermission didn't hold out.

No rain checks were asked or given. Once inside, the attractive gym, blazoning with multi-colored streamers, banners, and bright lights, beautiful with yellowing corn, sheaves of wheat and oats, cedars, willow boughs and branches of fragrant sassafras, the weather was forgotten. In one corner stood an arbor with a fortunately dusky interior; in another a replica wigwam likewise dimly illuminated; in a third, a screen planting of boxed cedars; in the fourth a refreshment dispensary built of heaped-up bales of straw; and between these last two, the ludicrous travesty of a country store, displaying ginghams, vegetables, cutlery and shoes, etc., the whole having a delightful suggestion of rusticity. The success of these decorations was due to the skillful planning and direction of Samuel Kogon, '30, Architect, Mr. Fiesser advising.

Manny Peitzman's Rustic Ramblers gave the urge, Keegler furnished the cookies, the ice cream was by Breyer's, punch by Sandburg costumes by Pitou, and lighting effects by Saltzgiver and Meyers; nitrogen furnished the atmosphere. A side-splitting farce by Coleman, Schwartz and Sherman hardly offered a breathing spell between halves. Everybody was dressed swell, everybody looked happy, things went over with a bang and kept banging away into the wee hours. Many alumni, all the faculty, lots of fellows, girls galore, the orchestra and no mosquitoes, attended.

Prizes went to Samuel Goldfarb and partner and Nathan Werrin and partner, as the two best-dancing couples on the floor. Mrs. Goodling was the very popular hostess to the girls. Most credit for the affair is due to President Steinberg, who gave his untiring effort toward its success, and to his classmates, the chef, Mr. Samuels and Mr. Stangel, who put his department at the Juniors' disposal.

M. A. G.

There will be a building adorning the campus in the near future which has long been regarded as necessary. The Mechanics and Administration Building is to be a combination of Georgian and Southern Architecture, according to Mr. L. H. Bailey, in charge of the work. It will be situated 120 feet from Lasker Hall and seventy feet from Elm Lane, with which it will be connected by a drive in the shape of an arc. The building will be 100 feet long and 45 feet wide, two stories high and will be finished in stucco.

The front part of the building will be one story higher than the rear because the rear will have one story below the surface. This space will be given over to large repair, woodworking, forge and stock rooms. The first floor will consist of a machinery demonstration room in the rear, the offices of the Dean and Mr. Samuels, plus the post-office in the front. On the second floor will be two classrooms and a large laboratory.

The floors will be of cement and the foundation also of concrete, which, along with a steel framework, and slate shingles, will make the building fireproof.

There will be a road from the shops at the rear of the building to the Home Farm, and also an elevator to make the transportation of machinery to and from the field and within the building itself as small a problem as possible.

In 1928 the number of abortions in our herd became quite large. A solution for that problem became imperative. At that time, Dr. Turner of Harrisburg suggested the present Maternity Barn. Lack of funds however, prevented any constructive action being taken.

MORRIS LASKER DOMESTIC HALL

Early this year, Dr. Fretz of Harrisburg, after studying the situation, also suggested that a separate barn be built in which to house all cows with calf, during a period of two weeks before and three weeks after calving. After the necessary time for making the plans, the barn was started, and in 40 days was completed.

The barn is of the half-monitor type and consists of ten box stalls in a row, each 10′ x 12′. Each stall is completely separated from the other by walls built to the ceiling. It is equipped with separate doors, windows, mangers (filled from the outside), drinking fountains and drainage.

A cow when placed in one of the stalls will be handled as little as possible, so as to keep down the spread of the abortion bacillus. Only one man will come in contact with any of the animals and he will have to take sanitary precautions.

Before being admitted back into the main herd, a blood test of the cow will be taken and sent to Harrisburg for analysis. If a negative reaction is obtained, the animal will be admitted; if positive she will be sent to the special abortion herd.

In this way we hope to rid ourselves of the "Bacillus Bang", the disease most dreaded by the dairyman.

As cold winds and snows close us out from our usual outdoor activities it will be good news to Farm School's Literature sharks to hear, that the Library has acquired a 26-volume set of the complete works of Joseph Conrad.

Besides the old favorites, as, "Youth", "The Nigger of the Narcissus", "The Rescue", "Lord Jim", there are "The Shadow Line", "Allmayer's Folly", "Chance", "Victory" and many others.

The thanks of the student body for this addition go to Mr. Hart Blumenthal who is in charge of purchasing the books for the library.

As this set is very expensive, because single copies cannot be replaced, it is hoped that Miss Churchman will receive the whole-hearted support of the Student Body in keeping them in as good condition as possible.

The Trials and Tribulations of a Reporter

This play is supposed to depict the actual method by which the material is collected and also give you a brief idea of what's what.

ACT I

TIME—6.28.
PLACE—Ulman Hall, Krause's Room.

YE EDITOR—Thank God!
KRAUSE—Well, what do you want now?
Y. E.—Some dope on the Senior Class.
KRAUSE—What's the matter, are you blind or deaf? Any one with the least amount of intelligence can see what the senior class is doing. If it wasn't for the senior class this place would be dead. The Year Book Committee is working like a well oiled machine. The pictures for the Year Book are expected to be in by the end of this month. With the seniors on the football team, the team should win every game this season. The old officers are still in place, now beat it.

ACT II

TIME—6.40
PLACE—Ullman Hall. Basement.

DOGON—What's the idea of dragging me out of the A.A.?
Y. E.—THE GLEANER will be out soon,

and we want the junior class in it for a change.

DOGON—If you've heard this one, stop me. The junior class after putting over the prom with a bang, does not rest on its laurels but hopes to be wearing its class sweaters all over the thriving metropolis of Doylestown in the very near future. We have our pennants and they are not bad, if you ask me. The football team is practically made up of juniors.

Y. E.—Yes, I've heard that before.

ACT III
TIME—6.45
PLACE—Campus.

Y. E.—Where have you been?
ROSEFELDT—Freshman class meeting.
Y. E.—Did you discuss much?
ROSEFELDT—Plenty. The banquet is coming along great. We're just waiting until we can stroll the campus without the traditional freshman adornments, namely, cap and tie. The class wishes to thank Mr. Marcus for his interest. Under the able guidance of Captain Gysling we hope to give the Juniors a little setback. We recently had elections of officers, with results as follows:

Goldstein—*President*
Lichtenstein—*Vice Pres.*
Nicholson—*Treas.*
Rosefeldt—*Sec.*

ACT IV
TIME—7.15.
PLACE—Brooder (*very appropriate*).

Y. E.—Hi Jerry, What's doing?
ARNOVITZ—Not a thing.
Y. E.—Anything doing in the poultry club?
ARNOVITZ—Well, after a pretty quiet summer, we're going to smoke this place up with a little steam. We took a trip with the Hort. Club to Vineland. The usual election of officers will take place in the very near future. A well planned program has been arranged for the winter months. You'll hear plenty about us then.

ACT V
TIME: After 7 p.m.
PLACE—Campus. First and second floors Ulman Hall.

MOSKOWITZ—Don't bother me now. Can't you see I'm in a hurry! I've got to get done before Mr. Fleming starts inspecting.
Y. E.—It'll only take you a minute to give me some information of the Hort. Club for THE GLEANER.
MOSKOWITZ—Oh! All right. But you had better walk beside me. I don't want to make too much noise. We took a trip to Trexler's Orchards which was only one of a series of pretty fine trips. As you know we've had movies quite often during the summer. We had elections of officers and all the old ones were retained except for our secretary, who wanted to give somebody else a chance and so I took his place. Boy! You know those officers must be pretty good if the most exclusive club in school keeps them.
Y. E.: I hear that most exclusive club bunk all over again.
FRANK: All right. Try to get a writeup next time.

ACT VI
TIME: Between 8 and 9 p. m.
PLACE: R. and R.'s room. First floor.

RUDOLPH: Come in if you're good-looking.
Y. E. (*so naturally I walked in*): What saying, Charlie?
RUDOLPH: Tennis Club coming along

with a racket. The club has balls which were new at the beginning of the season and they also played a match, which they never did before. So you know we've been progressing. The old officers have enough friends in the club to keep them in their places. The condition of the courts at the present time will speak for the activities of the club. As I was saying, Bennie——

Y. E. (*A psychological insight told me I'd better beat it.*)

ACT VII

TIME: Between 9 and 10 p. m.
PLACE: Somewhere in the school.

Y. E.: Hey Dutch, com'ere a minute!

WERST: The band looks like a million dollars. And when we play at the Doylestown Fair, Football Games and Philmont Country Club this year, it's going to be mean??? The freshmen have a fine turnout. We have substitutes for every instrument. In case any of the upper-classmen get disgusted with life, the band can go on. That's about all now, but you'll hear plenty from us during football season.

ACT VIII

TIME: During the still hours of the night.
PLACE: S. Marcus' room, Lasker Hall.

S. MARCUS: What's the idea waking a guy up this hour of the night?

Y. E. (*very timidly*): Well, you see, I'm a co-editor of THE GLEANER and——

S. MARCUS: To be or not to be, it ain't? You want a writeup on the Senate. Fortunately for some and unfortunately for others the famous Senate has not been in session for the past two months. All due to the excellent deportment and extraordinary co-operation of the entire student body in observing the school laws. You might as well get the Council dope now. The Council's last

dance was the alumni dance, which was run off in the usual well oiled fashion. The next dance will be the Hallowe'en dance. The Council ran all the social activities at the Faculty Picnic. We have appointed a reception committee to take care of the visiting football teams. The dances will be K.S. if you only bring out the girls.

ACT IX

TIME: Three-Time Milking.
PLACE: Dairy.

SHIPMAN: Where you going?

Y. E.: Just came down to look the place over.

SHIPMAN: You're editor of campus news, aren't you?

Y. E.: Uh huh!

SHIPMAN: Here's a writeup you forgot to get. The Dairy Club has started to function. At the first meeting the dairy seniors were elected as charter members and they elected the following officers: Gysling, President; Smiel, Vice-President and Shipman Sec. They drew up a constitution and a membership committee was appointed and quite a few candidates were handed in. We expect to visit the large dairy farms in this section. And I wouldn't be surprised if we have a judging team at the Eastern States Exposition before long.

ACT X

TIME: 5 a. m.
PLACE: Details Dairy.

Y. E.: Take cow No. 30 next, Phil.

KLEINMAN: Fat chance.

Y. E.: Say by the way, give me the Varsity Club writeup.

KLEINMAN: Give somebody else No. 30. With the summer months at a close the Varsity Club has again become an active organization. The Varsity Club proposes to take charge of all pep meetings and is also taking charge of all football tickets which will be sold in the future. The Varsity Club is mainly responsible for that certain feeling which is predominating on the campus—you know, "that football feeling." That's all I have to say, we've never said much; our actions speak for us.

Talking about Carlyle's "Hero and Hero Worship", we would call Sam Wattman's attention to his need of studying same.

Funeral services for Mr. Abraham Erlanger were held at the School, coincident with the family services in New York. The student body and members of the faculty gathered in the reception room of Lasker Hall where Mr. Erlanger's portrait hangs. In front of this portrait, which was draped in black crepe, rested a floral design, prepared by the Floriculture Department.

Mr. Samuels opened the services with the Consolation to Those in Mourning. Dean Goodling then told of the wholehearted interest in Farm School affairs which the deceased had; what a heavy strain the campaign in 1926 had been on him; how, because of ill health he was unable to become a frequent visitor to the School; how deep his interest in Farm School remained to the end. Mr. Stangel referred to Mr. Erlanger's fortunate appearance as one of a group of leaders on the death of Dr. Krauskopf and spoke of his democracy and personal interest in those carrying on the daily work of the School. Several of the farms and the development of the Dairy were due to Mr. Erlanger's beneficence. A concluding prayer was given by Mr. McKown.

———

Taxi Driver—"Where to?"
Drunk—"None of your business!"

MY IDEA IS THIS

We are people in these United States specially gifted with a good dose of freedom and are looked upon as an example of perfect progress.

But are we worthy of any such acclaim, considering the attire men step into when the thermometer registers 95° in the shade? We are sensible, some say. Are we? when our brothers, or call them what you will, in Jungleland dress according to Nature's dictates?

What we need are fewer and cooler clothes in summer. Something more suitable than Pajamas, however.

We need a martyr to the cause, one who will not flinch under the police officer's icy stare, and who will strut down Main Street in close communion with the elements. (Without getting a bump on his cranium.)

———

Who's Who

She's always with the boys,
And never does complain.
She walks to her domain,
No matter if it shine or rain.
Her library is her work!
A hustling fellow; she doesn't shirk.
No one who loafs does she like.
The chirp of birds, does she know,
And names the flowers as she goes.
She greets a fellow with "Joe" or "Ben".
She says, "I hope you're well again."
We bid her well, down in our hearts.
God bless Miss Churchman for her pains!
Her work for us is not in vain!

———

"Fools ask questions wise men can't answer."
"Yeah, that's why I failed my last exam."

———

"May I have the last dance with you?"
"You've just had it."

Campus Chatter

"First-Class Destruction Work Done.—See Bailey." Wonder how our Campus will survive its facial operation? Note to Alumni: Surprises await your coming next Alumni Day.

Farm School annex at the Jewish Hospital will soon close up for all the patronage we've been giving it lately. Appendix removals have practically gone down to zero. Our best wishes for a speedy and complete recovery go to Rogalski, Jacobson and Michaels, all of '32. Upper classmen hereby showing their superior wisdom.

THE GLEANER IS PLEASED TO ANNOUNCE THE ELECTION OF EMANUEL PETKOV, '30 AND ALEX. KRICHEFF, '32, AS ASSOCIATE CAMPUS NEWS EDITOR AND ASSISTANT ART EDITOR RESPECTIVELY. WATCH US STEP!!!!!

New Contributions show that interest in things literary is not missing at Farm School. The Staff wishes to thank Moscowitz, '30, and Smith and Rosenzweig, '32, for their efforts in helping to publish a better GLEANER. There's still room for more, so don't give up.

Time to think of the corn picking for the Fair, boys! 'Member last year?

THE FARM SCHOOL BAND THIS YEAR AGAIN OCCUPIED THE PLATFORM DURING THE DOYLESTOWN FAIR. ITS RENDITIONS, BECAUSE OF SINCERE AND PERSISTENT PRACTICE, FURTHER ENHANCED ITS GOOD NAME.

Thanks go to the Greenhouse Squad and "Headgear" Hartenbaum for keeping the lawn flower beds as spots of beauty, all summer long.

Seniors will soon feel like applying the brakes to Father Time's chariot.
The last finishing touches—the Senior Classes—are at hand.

THE HARVEST GOOD TIME MENU WAS GIVEN A GOOD START WITH THE STAGING OF THE FACULTY PICNIC, AUGUST 29. THE JUNIOR PROM HELPED IT ON, COURSE WILL BE IN THE FORM OF THE ANNUAL CORN SHOW.

Milton "Buck" Werrin, Editor-in-Chief, is somewhere in the Adirondacks, recovering from an illness. The Staff says, "Take it easy, Buck."

Now that the Season's started, let's get that old coordination—cooperation, or whatever it is . . . At Farm School we call it "Fight".

WHO'S WHO

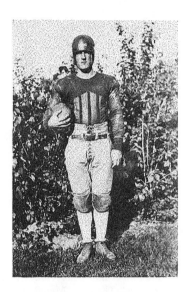

ALFRED GYSLING

SAM MARCUS

"Al" came to N.F.S. from Glen Nor High, the source of many other football stars on Farm School's teams in the past. His wealth of experience in that game during his stay at Glen Nor made him a valuable asset to the teams on which he played, both in his Freshman and Junior years. In both these years he won his letters. This year finds him Captain at Farm School.

Gysling is not much on chattering. He lets his actions speak for him. But on the field or at his work, whatever it may be, you know that he's there.

As captain of the football eleven, he is a future member of the A.A. Board. Besides this office he has been Vice-President of his Freshman Class and is at present Vice-President of the Varsity Club, and President of the newly formed Dairy Club. Dairying is his Project.

His quiet, steady ways have won him many good friends.

"Al" thinks that we've a good fast team this year. Although his being on the line will not place him in the limelight, as much as other captains, still we know that the hole he fills at guard and the moral support he gives to the team will be worth a gold mine to Coach Samuels!

If you don't know it, you're looking at a fighter. Guts and aggressiveness have helped Sam make a name for himself at Farm School.

As a Freshman, he was on the baseball and basketball teams, and on all major class committees. Besides this he organized the present Poultry Club.

He took part in his Junior Class Baseball and Basketball games, and served on the major committees again. He was President of the Poultry Club and on the membership Committee of the Horticulture Club.

His popularity has far from diminished at the beginning of his Senior Year, for he holds the position of Vice-President of the Student Body and Vice-President of his class. With these duties he has also to perform those connected with the offices of the Secretary of the Senate and Student Council. And on top of these he manages to find time to be Exchange Editor of THE GLEANER, Vice-President of the Poultry Club, Secretary of the Horticultural Club and Senior Adviser to the Class of '32.

Poultry caught his fancy early in his stay as Farm School and he has stuck to it ever since. His characteristic fighting spirit has helped him to get the most possible out of his work in class and out. He's had a constructive career at Farm School, and with good chances we will hear much of Sam in the future.

A. RELLIS, '30

Alumni Notes

Max King Steinberg, '28, is at Walker Gordon.

I. B. Ibaugh, '01, is Manager of Farms at State Hospital.

Archie Cohen, '27, is to be married in December. Congratulations, "Old Bean." And more good news, he's purchased a farm at Buckingham, Pa.

Joe Kovarick is connected with Walker Gordon.

O. Bing Myers, '29, is a Nurseryman in West Chester, Pa.

H. Dubrow, '29, is with Davey's Tree Surgeons. He expects to enter Cornell.

Goodstein, '29, has entered Mass. Aggie.

Wolfson, '27, was married in September in New York City. Lots of luck.

"Morphy" Weshner, '29, is a dairyman at Pottsville, Pa.

Edgar Hesch, '21, florist, in Philadelphia, has remodeled his store and seems to be prospering.

Lipson, Beck and Silver are at Freehold, N. J. Still going strong.

Harry Hurevitz has returned from California and is now connected with the greenhouse of Thomas, Menghorn and Company in Philadelphia.

Solis, '27, came back from California.

Zaroe, '29, is on a Poultry farm in California.

Emile Rivkin, '29, is at his Uncle's ranch in California.

Catherwood is on an intensive vegetable farm in Southern N. J., in charge of sales of Produce. Good prospects.

Nerlinger, '28, has formed a connection with a dairy farm near Paoli, Pa., and is in charge of a small herd.

Wm. Wolfson, '27, was married September 8 to Miss Dorothy Goldstein of West New York, N. J. Harry Rabinovitz, '25, was best man. Other former schoolmates present were: Sam Price, Harry Semel, Elmer Wiseman, Herman Litwin, Isadore Levin, Dave Brandt and Harry Bachman. According to the latter, there was plenty of real Farm School atmosphere and cheers.

Butch Rosen has entered P.M.C. as Cadet Rosen.

"Dutch" Jung is at Norristown State Hospital as Farm Manager's assistant.

Essrig is acting as assistant dairy manager at the State Hospital.

Becker is in a Danbury (Conn.) greenhouse.

"Polly" Pollachek is at Chapel, Pa., as Manager of Rising Sun Stock and Dairy Farm.

Tankenbaum dropped in recently. He can be found at 1121 Morrison Ave., Bronx, New York.

Hoguet has entered "Penn. State".

CHICAGO CHAPTER N. F. S. ALUMNI

Our first meeting and dinner of the new season was held at the Hotel Sherman. With our list of grads increasing the attendance grows and with the new members added interest.

The Chicago Chapter was well represented at the old school. Five members— a good showing from this goodly distance! Until the small hours of the morning the story of "A NEW FARM SCHOOL" was told by these travelers to a really interested group, many of whom have been away from the school twenty years.

President Carl H. Kahn has been appointed a National Committeeman. President Kahn took a few reels of pictures at the school which were splendid.

WALTER P. MORRIS, '22.

"That Iodine Blonde there reminds me of the ocean."

"How do you figure that?"

"She looks green but she acts rough at times."

"At last I have found her out!" cried the excited lover, as the maid told him his sweetheart was not in.

NEW YORK CHAPTER

TO THE EDITOR OF THE GLEANER:

During the summer we have been inactive, but by the time THE GLEANER goes to press we shall have resumed our meetings. If you see fit, you can mention the fact that we shall be more firmly banded together this year and shall try to cooperate with the other chapters to increase our activities in the behalf of Farm School, as well as attract those graduates who have been taking only a passive interest in our organization. At present I have only a few social items which may be of interest.

William Wolfson, '27, was married on the 8th of September in Union City, N. J.; H. Rabinowitz, '25, acted as best man. Many of Wolfson's classmates attended.

Carl Schiff, '27, is to be married on September 21st to Miss Claire Weinberg of New York City—Schiff is landscaping for the City Park Department.

Mark Goldstein, '25, and University of Florida, '29, has established residence in New York. He is with a brokerage house. He denies having abandoned an agricultural career and claims that he daily associates with Bulls, Bears and Lambs.

Sam Colton, '26, abandoned a desk and portfolio in the city and returned to the soil. He is with a poultry plant in New Jersey.

Dr. Bernhard Ostrolenk, former Dean, is in New York, as Editor of the *Analyst*, a supplement of the *New York Times*.

This is all the information I have for the present. As I stated previously, we have been inactive as an association for the summer and I was able to keep in touch with only a few.

After our first meeting, I shall have a better letter for you.

HARRY RABEN,
Secretary, New York Chapter.

S. Marcus, '30

SCHOOL days again have resumed their usual rôle in our educational career. To a numbered few has befallen the opportunity to edit their school magazine and continue to hold fast the bonds of friendship with other schools. To me, a school publication is the "School's Encyclopedia of Progress." We consider a school magazine in the same light as a beautiful shrub in bloom. Its attractiveness must be attributed to prudent management, care and pruning out of the undesired wood in order that it may continue to prosper and retain its characteristics. The thoughts expressed in the various exchanges are our editorial guide and information station. Through them we learn how to retain and conserve the desired characteristics of a school magazine and yet strengthen our agricultural motive and progress with a steady, firm gait.

It is our hope that the editors of the various school publications with which we have formed relationships, will continue to strengthen our friendship through service and regular response.

PRESIDENT'S ADDRESS TO STUDENT BODY AND FACULTY

(Continued from page 17)

To the President and Dean of The National Farm School,

Philadelphia, Pa.

"GENTLEMEN:

"I am speaking for several other mothers, as well as myself, who have sons in your School, asking you, if you will not look into certain disagreeable, and to our minds, unmanly actions taken by the upper classmen against the 1929 Freshmen. .

"Being fully aware of the high position this Institution holds, particularly with the Jewish communities throughout the Nation who subscribe towards its maintenance, and further aware of the high ideals of its revered founder, Dr. Krauskopf, we cannot but feel that the hazing and raiding are surreptitiously carried on without your knowledge.

"The boys I have in mind are manly, endeavoring to the best of their ability to keep their promise made to you when you were considering their application. Knowing the spirit of our sons, I beg to assure you, this plea comes from the mothers and not the sons, because we suffer when they do—in silence. We learn that their eyes have been tied; their nightclothes taken off, and that they have been beaten up by the upper classmen. It may be fun for the instigators, but I assure you, the Freshmen become nervous when thus tortured. Hence, the good work your Institution is endeavoring to carry out, at a great amount of money, energy, and good intent, is nullified.

"I am fully aware, that a certain amount of school spirit is necessary in institutions and colleges, but surely this can be carried out innocently, instead of brutally, as has been the case at your School. Many of your lads are of a refined, non-aggressive nature, and all mothers who know their sons, suffer even more than the boys themselves when they are needlessly tortured.

"My husband and I are highly pleased and grateful that our son, who is a Freshman, has this opportunity for a free course at your School. He loves the open, and is ambitious to make some branch of agriculture his future vocation, and given this great opportunity, it is our sincere prayer, he may graduate and not be driven away from the School he loves by the rough treatment which now prevails.

"Hoping you will pardon my taking so much of your valuable time, I am,"

From such indiscreet and silly happenings, for which some of you are responsible, what did you accomplish? You disgusted the victims and gave heartaches to their mothers. This is not construction, it is destruction; and I appeal to your manhood and common sense to cut the word "Hazing" from your vocabulary substituting that of "Good-Fellowship".

I am giving good advice, especially to the Freshmen who next year will become Juniors; at the same time, I am telling you what will happen if you fail to follow this advice. I know at heart you are good fellows—would rather follow the right than the wrong path, so if you want to please your Trustees, Teachers and President, just buckle down to good teamwork, working and playing harmoniously together.

Thus you learn through the President of the Board of Trustees their decision, that they stand back of the Dean and Faculty to stamp out hazing at The National Farm School.

On two previous occasions I spoke to the student body, asking them to abandon this practice, without effect. I shall not do so again. Let the 1929 Freshman Class remember this caution when they become the Juniors of 1930.

DEFINITIONS

Coincide—Cohen and Levy had a fight, but I took coincide.

Analyze—Anna says she doesn't pet, but analyze.

Disguise—Disguise been after me all day.

Omniverous—Omniverous happy sober, as drunk.

Satiate—I took my girl to a dinner and I'll satiate everything.

Judicious—I like Gefilte fish and other judicious. .

EXTRACTED HONEY

(Continued from page 13)

not granulate so readily as that which has this sugar in a larger proportion. It should be mentioned that levulose is always the predominating sugar. To bring granulated honey back into its liquid condition, it must be heated in a double walled boiler (top off) to 150 degrees Fahrenheit for 24 hours, until all crystals have disappeared. Honey may be placed on a stone in a container of water raised on supporters so that a complete circulation of water is possible. To keep honey in a liquid condition, it must be placed in a warm, dry room about 70 degrees Fahrenheit.

Extracted honey put on the market is absolutely pure, and free from any adulteration. The Pure Food Laws which went into effect Feb. 1, 1907, have remedied the adulteration of liquid honey by prohibiting the adding of a commercial invert sugar, glucose, used by many bottlers up to the enforcement of the law. By the addition of glucose, the bulk was increased greatly, thus bringing in more profits to the honey bottler. Glucose in the U. S. has been manufactured from corn starch, and in Germany from potato starch.

FRANK MOSKOVITZ, '30·

OUR 32ND HARVEST

(Continued from page 12)

muscles more than they should have, but they are none the worse for it. All jobs have their disagreeable ends and you've got to be man enough to withstand such 'hardships'."

General work in the Nursery consists in keeping the place clean of weeds; also, some replanting. They have some small jobs on hand now and are partly occupied. The No. 9 farm is being cared for by our Landscape department. Some pruning has been done and all hedges have been clipped. The Privet, Lombardy Poplars, Sycamore Cuttings and Rhododendron seedlings are doing well. They have replanted 1000 three-year-old hemlocks which will offer quite a return in the near future. Plants will be wintered in the beds. So much about Landscape.

As to the Apiary, nothing new is taking place in their department, but we will let you know more the next time we meet.

Mr. McKown—"When was the Revival of Learning?"
Earlbaum—"Just before the exam."

THE GLEANER

Is another school magazine
printed by

WESTBROOK
PUBLISHING CO.

CPSIA information can be obtained
at www.ICGtesting.com
Printed in the USA
BVHW04*1052170918
527708BV00015B/2142/P